For my teachers, all of y

How to Reduce Suffering and Increase Happiness: A 21 Day Meditation Challenge

Meditation has been used as a technique to reduce suffering and increase happiness for thousands of years. It's survival and increasing application today is a demonstration of its usefulness for millions of people over thousands of generations. Whether you're new to meditation or someone who has been practicing for decades, I guarantee you'll learn something new in this book. In addition, the lessons garnered from meditation are so layered that even when we think we know something, we discover our understanding was superficial and can go much deeper. This is why we call it a meditation practice, because there's no performance or achieving, there's just the practice.

With this book you'll embark on a "21-day Meditation Challenge." Research has demonstrated that it takes three weeks to form a new habit, so if you commit to meditating every day for the next twenty-one days you can develop what might become the best habit of your life.

Roadmap

The next twenty-one days are broken down into three sections corresponding to each week. In the first week we cover the fundamentals and build the foundation for a lifelong meditation practice. We'll discuss breath awareness, the benefits to a consistent meditation practice, letting go of stress in the body, how to use your meditation to practice presence, the importance of a beginner's mind, how to let go of thoughts, and we will practice not judging bodily sensations as a means to free ourselves from judgment. In this first week each meditation session is ten minutes, broken into two five minute sections with a brief mid-point check in.

In the second week we move deeper into our exploration of the body in order to question dominant paradigms and the way we currently perceive reality. We'll examine vulnerability, impermanence, desire and how it can create suffering, and interconnection versus separation. We'll question enlightenment, explore the value in suffering, and embrace purposelessness to find greater presence in the moment. During this phase we build from the foundation of week one and lengthen our meditations to twenty minutes. Again, they're broken in half with a brief mid-point check in.

In the third and final week we build from the previous two weeks, pushing ourselves and our meditation to thirty minutes. An empirical study found that meditators who meditated for an average of twenty-seven minutes per day changed the physical structure of their brains. More on that later, but it's amazing that we can change the structure of our brains through neuroplasticity just from sitting still and working on our focus!

Having completed two weeks of consistent meditation, in the third week we use our meditation practice as training to reduce suffering and increase happiness, for both ourselves and others. We'll cover the cultivation of listening, training not to think, feeling whole and perfect exactly as you are, how to work with your dark side or shadow, and how to take responsibility through choice. We'll experience non-duality in the body to see it everywhere, and we'll sidestep that pitfall of self development when we begin to perceive ourselves as better than others.

Using the body to understand reality

One reason why a meditation practice is so powerful is that we begin to understand complex concepts in the body. Once we experience something in the body, we become experientially familiar with it, leading to an understanding much deeper than the purely intellectual. For example, in one session you'll experience the connection between your mind, body and breath. This internal appreciation of interconnection will then enable you to better understand interconnection externally. Once you understand it in your own body, you see and feel it everywhere. This is the power of this type of practice over intellectual or cognitive understanding or discussion. If you haven't directly experienced it, then you don't know if it's true. A meditation practice gives you the tools to find the answers within yourself, rather than relying on an external source.

The structure

Each chapter follows the same structure which you'll quickly become familiar with. It begins with the key lesson for the daily session, relates the material to previous sessions, explains the day's concept, provides a mid-point check in after either five, ten, or fifteen minutes depending on the week, suggests how you can continue to apply the lesson throughout your day when not meditating, and ends with inspirational quotes to keep you motivated.

Most of us understand the power of stories so they're used frequently in the book. You might come to find that it's the stories that motivate you, and what you remember the most.

The first time you follow through the twenty-one days it's recommended you experience them sequentially, as they're ordered in complexity. But after your first complete program, you can freely pick and choose which individual sessions you'd like to revisit.

Many readers also find the audio version of this book helpful. Complete with a custom soundtrack, these recorded sessions range in time in accordance with the weekly schedule described above.

The basics

Step one to establishing a meditation practice is to commit to do it every day. There's a saying that if you miss one day in meditation it costs you a week of progress; miss a day and lose a week. For the next three weeks, do it, and don't waiver. After that you'll have established a new habit that is guaranteed to improve your life.

It's recommended that you establish a daily routine to meditate. Research into habit formation has found that context is more important than willpower. Create the context for meditation by doing it at the same time every day, in the same room, with the same cushion and blanket, or chair. You'll find that the creation of a consistent context will help to deepen your meditation practice and create sustainability.

The time of day is up to you, but most people prefer the morning because they're well rested and not at risk of falling asleep, and they have the mental capacity for sustained focus. It's recommended you meditate on an empty stomach so that you're alert, and that there are as few distractions as possible.

You can choose from many postures for meditation, such as any comfortable seated position, including sitting in a chair. You might sit on a cushion cross-legged, or with your legs out, against a wall or not, with your hips slightly higher than your knees to reduce any pressure on your knees. Your hands might be folded on top of each other, or flat on your knees, thumbs touching. Eyes may be closed, or slightly open and looking down, and so on. You can also lay down although many people will tend to fall asleep if they do so. Rather than delineating all the available postures, it's recommended that you experiment with a few, find out which works best for you, then stick to it. The best posture for you is the one in which you're most comfortable, as this will minimize distractions. Experiment as much as you need, move if your legs go numb, scratch an itch if you need to. Eventually find the posture that suits you and stick with it.

In a nutshell, to properly set up your meditation practice you should seek to minimize distractions, whether they're coming from noise outside of you, bodily sensations like pain, or the mental wanderings of your mind (by far the biggest source of distraction). Every now and then you won't be able to avoid external or internal noise, and that's fine, it's part of the practice. If the noise is external you can either move to a new location to meditate or accept it as a challenge to stay for the entire session.

You're all set

Now that we've covered the basics we can move into our first session. It's normal to feel a mix of excitement and fear for what you're about to do, but if you complete each meditation session, you'll learn to reduce your own suffering and increase happiness, in just twenty-one days.

Day 1

Breath Awareness

The key lesson in today's session is that your breath is an underutilized and limitless resource for presence.

Our breath is always with us. Unfortunately, this often means we take it for granted. Take a few moments and imagine what it would be like if you were unable to breath. You might even hold your breath. Notice how quickly panic sets in. Now deepen your breath, a deep invigorating inhalation, matched with a corresponding deep and easeful exhalation. Notice how your state of mind changes just from deep breathing. Notice any tension in the body and let it go each time you breathe out. Continuing this process, become aware of both how much tension you're holding in your body, and how much you can deepen your relaxation.

The word 'spirit' originates from the Latin *spiritus*, which means breath. Your breath is literally your spirit; nourish it during this meditation. Take five minutes now and do nothing else but enjoy your breath. There's no need to enforce a depth of breath, just natural breathing without effort. Just your breath, nothing else.

Mid-point check-in

Inevitably, our minds wander, whether one is new to meditation or has been doing it for years. Each time your mind wanders, patiently and persistently come back to the breath without judgment. Instead of being frustrated with your wandering mind, be encouraged each time you catch it wandering. This is progress! Don't allow the mind to distract you with supposedly more important things to do, checklists, emails, messages, work, family. You give enough of your time to these things, don't give them this time. There is nothing more important for you to do right now. Just pay attention to your breath for another five minutes.

Here's how you can apply this lesson to the rest of your day

Throughout the day, repeatedly come back to your breath. Even when talking with someone, watching TV, working, try to keep some awareness of your breath. At the end of the day when you go to bed reflect on how it went and how it made you feel, to finally give your breath the attention it deserves, even if just for a day.

Parting quote

"Flowers in the springtime, Autumn's moon, breezes in the summer, winter's snow—If your mind is not filled with useless things, those days are your best." – Mumon Ekai

Day 2

Benefits to Meditation According to Modern Science

The key lesson in today's session is that modern scientific research can help motivate us to meditate.

Building from the last session, you've already become more aware of your breath. At some point during your meditation practice you're likely to question: "Why am I doing this? Should I be spending my time on more productive things?" To help you stay motivated, in this session we briefly discuss some of the benefits of a consistent meditation practice without giving you too many details or descriptions of specific studies.

Practical benefits of a regular meditation practice found in peer-reviewed research include the following: It helps to reduces anxiety, increase self-esteem, increase empathy, and increase trust. Meditation can improve memory as it physically alters the structure of our brains increasing grey matter density in the hippocampus, known to be important for learning and memory, and in structures associated with self-awareness, compassion, and introspection. Take a moment to appreciate that you're changing the structure of your brain as you meditate.

Research has also found that experienced meditators had a thickening of the cerebral cortex associated with attention and emotional integration. Cortex translates as bark, as the outermost part of the brain. It limits your natural instincts, and so you can understand your meditation practice as training to inhibit your most basic responses.

In summary, meditation will help you become more peaceful, less reactive, and less defensive. It will also help you to awaken to the beauty and awe that continuously surrounds you, finding the extraordinary in the ordinary.

Continue with the previous session and focus on your breath and nothing else. Don't give your attention and time to anything else right now. Focus on your breath for the next five minutes, improve your self-awareness, compassion, and introspection, and change the structure of your brain.

Mid-point check-in

Take a moment to check in with your mind, where is it? Come back to your breath. Stay there as long as you can over the next five minutes.

Here's how you can apply this lesson to the rest of your day

Your meditation practice doesn't stop after your sit. Today try to recognize all the opportunities available to work on your practice. For example, how often can you be aware of your breath? While washing dishes, Thich Nhat Hanh talks about mindfully caring for each dish as though it were a baby in a bath. Challenge yourself to still your mind every time you walk up or down stairs. Can you keep a clear mind while folding laundry? Can you listen to someone without thinking of what you're going to say next? Can you stay focused on them and what they're saying without allowing your mind to wander? Really enjoy your food. Eat slowly, and don't prioritize other things, such as TV, emails, your phone, or conversation, over the joy and pleasure to be found in eating. Even when going to the washroom, can you maintain your focus?

Parting quote

"Who has ever learned to ride by talking about horses? If you wish to follow the Path, enough talking! Do it!" - Lao Tzu

Day 3

Letting go of Stress in the Body to Find Ease

The key lesson in today's meditation is to relax the body, which will in turn contribute to a calm mind.

Building from previous sessions you have now learned about the benefits of meditation and may have been able to experience some of these simply by focusing on your breath. The breath is a powerful link between our physical reality and our state of mind, and simple exercises that focus on the breath are used in a wide variety of fields to help with anxiety, stress, focus and athletic performance, to name a few. The breath is the core physical focus of your meditation practice, but sometimes it can be hard to experience fully when other physical distractions are in the way. You may notice yourself fidgeting, repeatedly attending to an itch, or continuously readjusting your posture to make yourself more comfortable. Don't worry, this is completely normal, and you will see these distractions fall away the more you practice. Today, our focus will be on letting go of stress in the body which will make it easier to sit in stillness and calm the mind.

Follow the breath, in and out the nose. Feel the air at the tips of your nostrils. Notice your stomach, rising and falling. Now, bring your attention to your toes, and start to let go. Slowly work your way up the feet, and up your legs, releasing every muscle as you go. Make your way up through the pelvis and the midsection. Inhale into the stomach, then exhale, letting go of any stress and muscular tension that doesn't need to be there. Relax through your chest, and then gently bring your focus to the fingertips and relax your hands. Work your way up the forearms and upper arms, then release through your shoulders. Notice any tension in the neck and throat, and release. You may even feel your shoulders sink down as you let go. Follow the breath in the nose, nice and slowly, then back out. Bring your attention to the jaw and the inside of the mouth as you inhale, then let them soften as you exhale dropping the tongue from the roof of your mouth. Let the ears and eyes relax and notice any sensations as you relax all around your head, slowly moving to a single point on top of the head. Your whole body should be relaxed at this point, making it easier to bring focus to the breath. Keep following the air in and out the nose and feel the cyclic path it takes through the body for five minutes.

Mid-point check-in

If you notice the mind starting to wander, just gently redirect focus back to the breath. Follow it into the nose, into the stomach, and then back out. If you notice any tension building in the body, take an inhale, and use your exhale to gently let go.

Become aware of the softest, most relaxed part of your body. Allow it to inspire softness in the rest of the body. For the next five minutes allow it to spread.

Here's how you can apply this lesson to the rest of your day

Become increasingly aware of when you're unnecessarily holding tension in the body. This means bringing your awareness to your body regularly, then releasing tension with a deep exhale connecting mind, body, and breath.

Parting quote

"The miracle is not to walk on water. The miracle is to walk on the green earth in the present moment, to appreciate the peace and beauty that are available now." - Thich Nhat Hanh

Day 4

Practicing Presence Without an End Goal

The key lesson in today's session is to let go of a desired outcome or goal in your meditation practice as you begin to experience the joy of presence without desire.

Building from the last sessions start with three minutes of breath awareness. Devote all your focus to your breath. Let go of the desire for any goals or benefits, even though these exist. You're just paying attention to your breath, that's it.

Three minutes later: Here's a quote from the Indian classic the Bhagavad Gita, a book Gandhi read from every day: "Meditation is better than knowledge; Yet even better than meditation is the release of attachment to the fruits of our efforts. For peace immediately follows." In letting go of our egocentric goals during and outside of our meditation practice, we find freedom. But don't just believe the Gita, try it for yourself! Let go of any goal in your meditation practice, see if concentrated effort without attachment to a goal brings you freedom in this moment, and the next, and the next. Catch the mind every time it tries to insert a goal, then let it go with an exhalation. Work with this now for the next five minutes, you can keep your focus on your breath without seeking an end goal.

Mid-point check-in

Most of us are goal-oriented as this is celebrated in our societies. While there are clear benefits to setting goals, today, for a change, try something new, effort without a desired goal. Buddha was once asked how he crossed the river of everyday struggles to find freedom within every moment. He answered that when he tried too hard to swim across the river he would tire, sink and be swept away. And when he didn't try hard enough, he was forced to tread water continuously, where he would again tire, sink, and be swept away by the river of everyday suffering. It was only when he found balance between effort and ease that he crossed the river, Buddhism's middle path.

Pushing this analogy further…even if we obtain our goal on the other side of this river, whatever that goal might be, then what? Well, we find that the obtainment of the goal brings only temporary satisfaction, and that very quickly we're no longer content with that goal, we seek a new goal or a new spot along the river. Once arrived on the other side of the river, perhaps we see another spot, one with more shade, or one with more beautiful trees. Always seeking more and thus never content. How can we break this mental process of perpetual dissatisfaction that plagues humanity? We can hack our mental system by enjoying the swim without concern for what's on the other side of the river.

Find your breath if you've lost it and stick to it. You're not trying to get to the other side of a river; you're just putting effort into enjoying your breath and the current moment, regardless of where you might end up. Work on this for the remaining five minutes.

Here's how you can apply this lesson to the rest of your day

For the rest of the day move deeply into whatever experience you're having. Regardless of whether you label this as a pleasant, unpleasant, or a neutral experience, move deeply into it. Today, let go of all your goals, don't concern yourself with getting to the other side of the river. Realize that you have less control over the end than you do over the process. Just enjoy the swim. Before you go to bed evaluate how this worked or didn't work for you.

Parting quotes

"Satisfaction does not come with achievement, but with effort. Full effort is full victory." - Mahatma Gandhi

"As long as you are trying to improve yourself, you have a core idea of self, which is wrong practice." - Shunryu Suzuki

Day 5

Beginner's Mind

The key lesson in today's session is to maintain a beginner's mind, opening ourselves to all possibilities in the present moment.

Building off our last sessions you've already come to better appreciate the simplicity of breath awareness, perhaps loving and fully appreciating the spiritus origin, and that it's the breath that animates us and gives us life. You may also have experienced the freedom that comes from letting go of the dominating influence of goals, finding freedom in presence regardless of what you're doing.

We begin by examining how little we know. No matter what someone might tell you, we don't know what happens when we die, we don't know our purpose, we don't know why children get life threatening illnesses or conversely, why some seemingly cruel people prosper. When we look at the most fundamental questions of life and death, we must admit, we know less than we like to admit.

Consider the following story of Socrates when he visited the Oracle at Delphi, who told him he was the smartest man in all of Greece. Humble Socrates couldn't believe this to be true and set out to prove that it wasn't. He traveled throughout Greece and engaged in conversations to match his wit against others, as was the practice at the time. At the end of it all Socrates had to admit that the Oracle was correct, that he was in fact the smartest man in all of Greece, because he was the only one that could admit that he knew nothing.

Today, embrace your full intelligence by appreciating the many things you don't know, and just maybe, moving more fully into the concept that you possess a wisdom greater than the intellect. One that you can't explain, but that you can feel, and eventually become.

Observe your thoughts over the next five minutes. Notice how often you fall into familiar thought patterns, and how these limit your understanding and possibilities. Like a car driving in the winter, stuck in the ruts that every car drives in, unable to turn and get out onto new terrain. See that when you think you know, you limit what might be. Simply observe your thoughts with this perspective for the next five minutes.

Mid-point check-in

A Zen monk once had a student who thought he already knew everything. This frustrated the monk because the student wasn't open to any of the lessons. Exasperated but inspired, the monk told the student to come to his hut for tea. Once there, he mindfully made the tea, enjoying our metaphorical swim in the river as he did so. He then began to pour the tea into the student's cup. Only he didn't stop pouring. The student, seeing that his cup was overflowing looked frustratingly at the monk, then back to the cup, and finally said louder than he wanted, "Stop! Can't you see the cup is already full?" Softly the monk replied, "And so it is with you; I cannot pour anymore in because you're already full."

Empty your cup, so that it can be filled endlessly. Honestly observe your thoughts. See for yourself that often we think we know, but if we're honest we must admit we can't be sure, or we don't know. Every situation is unique and should be approached with an empty cup. You might also observe that when we continuously empty our cup, we also get to continuously enjoy filling it. An endless cup of tea! Honestly observe your thoughts for the next five minutes.

Here's how you can apply this lesson to the rest of your day

Throughout the day, notice that whenever you think you already know something you stop paying attention. Maybe you become aware of this habit during a conversation, where someone is talking about something you feel you know a lot about already. You stop paying attention and rob yourself of the ability for further knowledge. A full cup without room for more tea. Today work at emptying your cup, and find how fulfilling it is to be refilled, as though you get to enjoy endless cups of tea with the only consequence being that you learn new information continuously.

Parting quotes

"We work to become, not to acquire." - Elbert Hubbard

"All we can know is that we know nothing. And that's the height of human wisdom." - Leo Tolstoy

Day 6

Letting Go of Our Endless Thoughts

The key lesson in this session is to train yourself to let go of your thoughts so that you can create space for awe and joy. This takes practice and time, and it's very challenging when it comes to training the mind. Don't forget to enjoy the journey as you let go of the destination; don't get frustrated, you're just practicing!

Building from the last sessions, today we focus on letting go of thoughts and creating space where previously there was mental clutter.

Today in your meditation try this technique. Close your eyes and picture a big blue sky. No clouds, no birds, just blue. Imagine this as being analogous to your natural state of mind, spacious, empty, endless. When thoughts invariably surface, imagine that there are clouds passing through the sky. Just as you wouldn't try to throw a rope over a cloud and tie it down, don't do this to your thoughts. Let them, like clouds, float out of the sky without attachment. Attach to nothing, just watch the sky. Do this for five minutes.

Mid-point check-in

Two monks returning from the city and heading toward their monastery came across a familiar river with a strong current. Although they had crossed the river many times and felt confident in their ability to do so, a young, apprehensive woman stood next to them. Compassionately one of the monks offered to carry her to the other side of the river. The woman happily accepted, put her arm around the monk's neck, and he sure-footedly carried her across the tumultuous and ever-changing river.

Once on the other side, he gently put her down. The young woman thanked him and walked off in a different direction from the monks as they set off to their monastery. The monk that had carried the women maintained a clear mind so he could enjoy the splendour of all that surrounded him; the wind in the trees and across his body, the territorial birds talking, the abundant and carefree insects living their brief lives. The other monk however allowed his mind to be consumed by anger. It feasted on thoughts of the inappropriateness of his fellow monk carrying that young woman. It swam in a pool of intoxicating self-righteousness. All along he missed the wonders of the phenomenal world that surrounded him. Robbed of presence he bathed in toxic emotions surfacing from something that had already come and gone.

No longer able to hold his anger it bubbled out his throat and he surprised his fellow monk when he yelled, "How could you have carried that young woman across the river? We're not even supposed to touch women, let alone carry them. How could you have done that?" He accused, with more spittle than breath.

The other monk looked at his angry friend and found compassion instead of judgment. He patiently replied, "I left that woman on the riverbank; you're still carrying her."

Continue with the big sky mind meditation for the next five minutes. Don't carry any thoughts with you. Let them go, just as the monk did with the woman once they reached the other side of the river.

Here's how you can apply this lesson to the rest of your day

Two things to practice today. First, become aware of how often you repeat the same thoughts over and over. Become aware of how you carry the past in the present, and therefore never fully experience the present. Second, stop these recurring thoughts. Stop lamenting or rehearsing the past or fantasizing about a future that may never be. Today, catch yourself when you devote mental time and energy to repetition, and instead of repetition create space so that you can observe and enjoy the present.

Parting quote

"Man postpones or remembers; he does not live in the present, but with reverted eye laments the past, or, heedless of the riches that surround him, stands on tiptoe to foresee the future. He cannot be happy and strong until he too lives with nature in the present, above time." - Ralph Waldo Emerson

Day 7

Experiencing Bodily Sensations Without Judgment

The key lesson in today's session is that we can experience bodily sensations without labeling them as pleasant or unpleasant. That is, we can accept the experience as it is, without judgment. As we become aware and improve upon this internal process, we'll find we judge external things less as well.

In our last session we learned how to quiet the mind by picturing a big sky and we heard the story of the two monks crossing the river, one who enjoyed the walk to the monastery and one who was consumed by negative thoughts. In this session we extend our ability to quiet the mind as we seek to experience our bodily sensations without judgment. We'll learn to sit without aversion to what we might normally label as unpleasant, and to sit without attachment to what we might normally label as pleasant, all while keeping the focus within the body, which is where all sensations begin.

The word emotion derives from a Latin word which means 'to move out'. If you calmly and objectively maintain an internal focus you can feel that an emotion starts somewhere in the body. When we're unable to hold it because we don't like the sensation, we push it out and end up sharing it with others. This is particularly problematic with emotions like anger or jealousy, where our inability to hold them and the sensations they produce in our bodies result in us sharing negativity with those around us.

However, sensations can be perceived as neutral as you'll experience in this meditation session. As you experience sensations in your body during this session don't label or judge them. Do you have discomfort somewhere? Experience it without judgment. If you smell dead fish or manure, can you experience them fully without judgment? In some Buddhist colonies people are eager to be assigned to clean the washrooms because it allows them to work on this practice. Feel excited or happy? Can you experience it without perceiving it as positive, and thereby not attach to it?

Think of something that makes you happy. Can you locate the sensation of happiness somewhere in your body? Once you find it, hold your mind there and experience it without attachment or judgment until it passes. Take a few minutes to work on this.

Now think of something that makes you angry. Can you locate the sensation of anger somewhere in your body? Once you find it, hold your mind there and experience anger without immediately suppressing or forcing it out. This may be the first time you've actually experienced and held anger in your body. Hold it, without judgment, and learn that you can hold anger in your body, and you don't need to share it with others. Take a few minutes to work on this.

Finally, think of something that makes you sad. Can you locate the sensation of sadness somewhere in your body? Once you find it, hold your mind there and experience sadness without immediately suppressing or forcing it out, but also without succumbing to it. This may be the first time you've actually experienced and held sadness in your body. Hold it, without judgment, until it passes, and learn that you can hold sadness in your body, and you don't need to share it with others. Take a few minutes to work on this.

Here's how you can apply this lesson to the rest of your day

You will have many opportunities to work with the key lesson from today's session. When someone angers you, feel how the sensation of anger originates in the body, then develop your capacity to hold it. If you experience anger or any emotion typically labelled as negative, locate it in the body and observe it passively as you've already trained yourself to do in this session.

You can do the same with any emotion typically labelled as positive. We tend to be averse to so called negative emotions, and we tend to attach to so called positive emotions. Today, observe their neutrality, their impermanence, and work on your ability to fully experience emotions within your own body.

As you improve your ability to observe sensations neutrally, unfamiliar nuances may become apparent, like the difference between discomfort and pain, for example. In a further session will build on our ability to hold negative sensations and emotions in the body, and how loving them without attachment or aversion makes them dissolve.

Parting quotes

"What you see, ugliness or beauty, is your own reflection." - Rumi

"That all is as thinking makes it so - and you control your thinking. So remove your judgements whenever you wish and then there is calm - as the sailor rounding the cape finds smooth water and the welcome of a waveless bay" - Marcus Aurelius

This one is from Yoka Daishi, as we begin to uncover the root of our emotions and their causes:

"Let us take hold of the root and not worry about the branches--

The moon is serenely reflected on the stream,

The breeze passes softly through the pines,

Perfect silence reigning undisturbed-- what is it for?"

Week One Complete

You've made it through one week of meditation, congratulations! You've become increasingly aware of your own breath; you've learned some of the benefits to meditation discovered through modern science; you've learned to let go of stress in the body in union with your breath; you've experienced the joy of presence without desire for an end goal; you've come to the profound realization that you know very little of life's biggest questions and in accepting this you've found limitless possibilities; you've learned to let go of your thoughts so that you can be in awe of what surrounds you; and, you've learned to experience sensations in your body without judgment.

Perhaps you've already noticed that your daily meditation sessions are helping to reduce your suffering and increase your happiness. If not, don't despair, we're just getting started and many of the concepts described in the first week can take years to fully appreciate and understand. This is the beauty of a meditation practice without a goal; there's always more to learn, practice and enjoy. An endless cup of tea.

As we move into our second week be aware that it is often the hardest because the excitement from the first week may have dissipated and we don't have the light at the end of the tunnel that we'll get in the third and final week. We'll also question some of our fundamental beliefs, which can be scary at first, but will ultimately be freeing. Knowing this, establish your determination and motivation to complete week two. Commit to it now, and don't allow any excuses to keep you from your commitment.

In our effort to grow your meditation practice to 30 minutes to help you change the structure of your brain, in week two we increase the length of time from 10 to 20 minute sessions. Make sure you give yourself this time to move deeply into the seven meditation sessions for week two.

Keep it up, we've only just begun and some of the most incredible things to be learned from a consistent meditation practice are yet to come. In the second week you'll learn to question several paradigms you've likely used to understand the world, including your perception of vulnerability, impermanence, suffering, interconnection, enlightenment, and purpose. In this second week we move more deeply into our bodies where we develop our understandings or internal processes, and then extend these experiential insights to our comprehension of external reality.

Day 8

Becoming Comfortable with Vulnerability

The key lesson in today's session is to become comfortable feeling vulnerable so that we can maintain an openness to all experiences. Often, we view vulnerability as a liability, something to be overcome with strength. The reality is that we're always vulnerable and fragile whether we admit this to ourselves or seek to continuously project strength.

Building from the last session we will continue to find tolerance for and expand our capacity for discomfort as we did in the last session when we experienced anger and sadness in the body. It's not comfortable to be in a position of vulnerability. Today's meditation practice will teach you to sit with your vulnerability, giving you the courage to approach each day with openness rather than a walled off illusion of strength. You might envision an open heart versus one locked in a safe, protected but hidden and trapped.

If you look up synonyms for the word vulnerable, they include weak, helpless, exposed and defenseless. These synonyms demonstrate our societal and systemic bias against vulnerability. But what does it really mean to be vulnerable? It means you're alive, vulnerable to illness, death and separation at any moment. It doesn't mean you're weak or helpless, although it does leave you exposed. To admit and hold our state of vulnerability takes tremendous courage. It's the breaking of your heart, until it stays open. Do you have the courage to live with a broken heart, open to everything that comes your way in this moment? To close your heart to protect it is to rob yourself of the joys and sorrows of life.

Imagine yourself in the middle of a ferocious battlefield hundreds of years ago. Rather than running or fighting, to stop the fight immediately you decide to lay down on your back, fully exposed to all around you, not even bothering to defend yourself. Observe the sensations that arise in the body as you begin to feel your vulnerability. Observe the thoughts that come into the mind, but don't attach to them or push them away, let them float by like clouds in the sky as you've already trained yourself to do.

Sit with your vulnerability. Don't push it away. You might discover that you have an unlimited capacity to hold and love it. Today, you make the word and experience of vulnerability synonymous with courage. You're not fighting, you're not running, you're sitting or lying down seemingly unafraid of any danger even though our imaginary battle surrounds you. For the next ten minutes imagine this battle scene, feel your vulnerability, hold your awareness there, and learn that you can hold vulnerability in the body and mind, and don't need to fear it.

Mid-point check-in

We're always vulnerable, whether we know it or can admit it. Embrace your vulnerability without aversion, see for yourself, in this meditation, that you can hold it, and experience it rather than running from it. If you do get scared, open your eyes, see that you're safe, and when you're ready, get right back into the meditation. Take an additional ten minutes to get comfortable with a sense of vulnerability, but now also notice that being vulnerable isn't a sign of weakness, but of courage.

Here's how you can apply this lesson to the rest of your day

Notice all the times you close yourself from your current experience as protection from a perceived threat. These occurrences may not be as apparent as you think. Notice how your judgments of others are attempts at making you feel better about yourself and your choices. Notice that in judging someone you create distance between yourself and that person, creating a separation that protects you from feeling for them. You might envision this now as a closing of your heart rather than its opening.

Notice how vulnerable we all are. Pay particular attention to people you may normally perceive as strong. Can you see their vulnerability beyond the gossamer veil of strength? At any moment they could get into an accident and become disabled or die or lose someone they love. Can you see your own constant vulnerability? Once you see it, can you hold it without aversion? Does the recognition of the vulnerability of yourself and things around you, not just people but animals, trees, insects and nature, create a heartfelt love for things because they are so fragile? It's their fragility which imbues them with value. Today, let your vulnerability open you to the fragility within and outside of you, and finally perceive the tremendous value and awe that continuously surrounds you, all of which could be gone in an instant. To love without limit makes you vulnerable, and to do it anyway requires courage.

Parting quote

"Security is mostly a superstition. It does not exist in nature, nor do the children of men as a whole experience it. Avoiding danger in the long run is no safer than outright exposure. Life is either a daring adventure or nothing." - Helen Keller

Day 9

Recognizing Impermanence

The key lesson in today's session is that all things are impermanent, and by recognizing this we won't attach to impermanent things that give us pleasure, nor will we run from impermanent things that create suffering. Attachment to something that is bound to change will inevitably create suffering, and aversion from something that is bound to change is pointless.

Building from the last session we'll continue to place value on the present but add the recognition that all things are subject to change.

Also, we'll learn that creating attachments or aversions to things that are impermanent serve only to prolong our suffering.

Imagine a drinking glass, maybe you have one in front of you now. Perhaps this glass has been used by a family for 30 years before it falls to the floor and shatters. Eventually, the broken pieces smash even further, and return to the soil from which they came. What was the glass before its current shape? What is it after it breaks? Regardless of your answers, you'll notice that what it is, is continuously changing; it has no permanent shape or function. It's the same with you. You're in a constant transition from one state to another, with no permanent self.

To describe it seems obvious, but most of us aren't living it. We are constantly preoccupied with ourselves and our own happiness and suffering. We often become preoccupied with our current state failing, in that moment, day, week, year, or lifetime, to see that it's impermanent.

If we like something, the sensation it creates in the body makes us feel good, we seek more of it and create an attachment. If we don't like something, the sensation it creates in the body makes us feel bad, so we create an aversion. But if we really understood impermanence, we wouldn't create any attachments or aversions to things that are inherently impermanent. Things will change; we all know this. Attaching to something impermanent is bound to create suffering. Avoiding or running from something impermanent only prolongs our suffering when we inevitably face it again. Once we understand impermanence we can get to the root of our own suffering, and how we're often the very cause of it.

Buddhism's first Noble Truth is that life is suffering. It's suffering because we all get sick, age and die. The second Noble Truth is that there are causes to our suffering, primarily our desires and our ignorance. Think of society's attachment to youth and desire to look and feel young, something that no one can hold on to forever, and think of the suffering this attachment creates. This is just one example of how our attachments create suffering, and because we know everything is subject to change, our attachments are guaranteed to make us suffer.

Spend ten minutes now listening to your changing body. Hear and feel the movements and sounds of the millions of bacteria in your gut; the flow of blood throughout your body; the changes in your heartbeat and breath. Your body is never the same from moment to moment. Understand impermanence experientially in your body, and you'll begin to see it everywhere. This growing wisdom will free you from the creation of attachments and aversions, and the self-creation of suffering.

Mid-point check-in

Meditation master Achaan Chaa told the following story: "You see this cup? For me, the cup is both broken and not broken. Seeing that it's not yet broken but recognizing that this state is impermanent, I enjoy it more when I drink out of it. It holds my water admirably, sometimes even reflecting the sun in beautiful patterns. If I should tap it, it has a lovely ring to it. But when I put this glass on a shelf and the wind knocks it over or my elbow brushes it off the table and it falls to the ground and shatters, I say, 'Of course.' But when I understand that this glass is already broken, every moment with it is precious."

The recognition of impermanence gives us clarity, not just to avoid attachment, but it helps to imbue the present with value. Knowing that you will eventually die helps you give greater value to today.

Now that you're experientially familiar with impermanence in your body, you're aware, and have felt, that it's constantly changing. We'll spend the next ten minutes of our practice understanding how we create our own suffering. First, think of something that makes you happy. Notice that the sensation of happiness starts somewhere in the body. Keep your awareness there until the sensation of happiness passes. How do you feel when it's gone? If you created an attachment to the pleasant sensation, when it leaves learn how you created your own suffering. If you didn't create an attachment, when it leaves observe how there's no suffering, just passive acceptance.

Second, think of something that makes you upset. Notice that the sensation of feeling upset starts in the body. Keep your awareness there until the sensation passes. How do you feel when it's gone? If you were able to hold the unpleasant sensations in the body, you've just learned that you don't need to suppress or run from them, you can hold them and experience them. There's no need to avoid or avert an experience, because it's impermanent.

By the end of this practice you'll have become experientially familiar with impermanence and have made significant progress toward reducing your suffering and increasing your happiness. Freedom is found through the experience of your own body. Spend another 10 minutes aware of your constantly changing body paying particular attention to sensations that come and go.

Here's how you can apply this lesson to the rest of your day

Continue this practice by noticing the impermanence of everything around you. See how you create your own suffering by attaching or averting from things that are continuously changing. Then see how much more you value the present with the knowledge that it can't last.

Parting quote

"All things are like a dream,

a ghost, a bubble, a shadow;

Like a dewdrop, or a flash of lightning;

This is how they should be seen." - Buddha

Day 10

Your Desires Create Suffering

The key lesson in today's session is that our desires create suffering. Recognizing this, suddenly we can free ourselves from suffering in any moment. Once we admit that we cause much of our suffering, we have the power to change it. In contrast, if we believe that others are the cause of our suffering, they have the power to end it or keep it going. Why would you choose to give the power of your own suffering to something or someone else? If you're the cause of most of your own suffering, you can also be the cause of escaping it and finding happiness.

Building from our last session we continue to examine how we self-create suffering, and how freedom from much of our suffering is within our control and can therefore happen in an instant. In our last session we learned of the first two noble truths of Buddhism: that life is suffering, and that there are causes to suffering. In this session we ask: What are the root causes of our suffering? The answer we explore today is desire.

In the west our dominant paradigm is one of scarcity, where the more you get the less others receive, and greed is valued as an asset of entrepreneurial individuality. You may have heard that the Inuit have about a dozen words to describe snow, and over 60 to describe sea ice. This is a demonstration of the importance of snow and ice to their culture. Similarly, we have many words to describe excessive desire including but not limited to greed, avarice, esurient, hungry, desideratum, voracious, predatory, aggressive, rapacious, materialistic, grasping, covetous, selfish, egotistical, and insatiable. One word for snow, but perhaps as many as 20 for greed. Despite our large vocabulary for greed or desire, we tend not to understand its relationship to suffering.

There are many ways for you to understand the relationship between desire and suffering in your own body. Here are a few examples although you shouldn't limit your experience to these. Many people have damaged their knees trying to force their legs into a full lotus posture during meditation. Their desire for a specific, unnecessary seated position creates suffering. When you're mildly ill with a cold, your desire to be healthy can make the experience much worse. After all, we all need to slow down occasionally. It's your desire for things to be different than they are that creates your suffering, not the mild illness. In a yoga practice you might force yourself into a deep stretch out of a desire for greater flexibility. Should the yoga teacher ask you to hold the pose for an extended period, it's your desire for rapid gains in your flexibility that almost immediately creates suffering.

Ultimately, our desire stems from a failure to accept things as they currently are. In this session, with a clear mind observe desire as soon as it surfaces. It might arise after you experience a pleasant sensation in the body, and you desire more of it. Or perhaps the mind will wander, and when you snap out of it, you'll realize that you were daydreaming of a desire. Observe how the desire is a failure to accept things as they are. Accept things as they are right now, free yourself from the desire in this moment, and literally feel lighter in your body.

For the next ten minutes clear your mind and objectively observe desires as they surface as though you were an outside observer of your thoughts. See how your desires, no matter how big or small, are a lack of acceptance and that they create suffering. Then remove them from the root by accepting things as they are, and see suffering vanish. Observe the tremendous control you have over your own suffering.

Mid-point check-in

The Buddha reportedly told the following story: A man once crossed a desert without water. Arriving in a village parched and dehydrated, he asked a vendor for water. The vendor showed him a cup of cold, refreshing water, but warned the man not to drink it because it was meant for someone else and contained poison. Staring at the water, the man couldn't control his thirst and drank the water anyway, thinking "I'm so thirsty I will drink this water now to feel refreshed and suffer later." This is how we treat desire; we constantly give in to it despite knowing and being told that it will cause us suffering later.

For the next ten minutes continue to observe your desires as they surface. Build on your understanding of the relationship between desire and suffering, and how quickly you can reduce your suffering by accepting things as they are.

Here's how you can apply this lesson to the rest of your day

Today, notice all the times desire arises within you, but instead of giving in to it and drinking the poisoned water, resist it. Do this repeatedly, and see that every time you withstand your desire, it's easier to resist next time. Become increasingly familiar with the relationship between desire and self-created suffering. Conversely, if you can't help but give in to your desire, see for yourself that it doesn't bring you sustainable happiness.

Parting quotes

"Wherever there is a craving, there is pain; Quiet your craving and you are blessed." - Buddha

"Do not tarnish that which you have by desiring that which you do not" - Epicurus

"It is not the man who has too little, but the man who craves more, that is poor" - Lucius Annaeus Seneca

Day 11

Exploring Interconnection to Understand Reality

The key lesson in today's session is that everything in the world is connected, yet we often perceive things as separate. We can first begin to feel this interconnection in our bodies by connecting the mind, body, and breath. After we feel this connection internally, we can better understand it externally. This can help us overcome the false paradigm of separation that is at the root of our biggest problems today.

Building from the last session we'll continue to seek connection within and outside of ourselves as we begin to feel and understand that our paradigm of separation is incorrect and should be replaced with a new paradigm of interconnection.

Neuroscientists have discovered we possess empathy neurons, where we literally feel the pain of others. At the smallest level, quantum physics has discovered entanglement, where two particles are connected in that the spin of one particle can determine the spin of another particle, potentially light years away. Einstein called this "spooky action at a distance". For thousands of years, recorded in ancient texts, yogis have expressed interconnection using the term *Sankya*, translated as exact knowing, to tell us that true perception is one of interconnection. Similarly, Alan Watts called the belief in separation our greatest delusion. He questioned whether a flower and a bee should really be considered separate beings since both are dependent on each other for survival.

Modern scientists have found that the DNA between a person and any other person is 99.9% the same; between a person and a banana 50% the same; between a person and a fruit fly 61% the same; and between a person and a mouse 97.5% the same. This speaks to our common ancestry and continued connection.

Lastly, we've even come to understand that adding wolves back into an ecosystem can have dramatic ecological effects, including changing the shape of rivers by altering the behaviors of the herbivores on which they prey. Think of this level of interconnection, where wolves can inadvertently change the shape of rivers!

Our belief in separation has grave consequences. At the root of the greatest threats facing humanity is the belief in separation, that because I'm separate from you, I can prosper and you can suffer, but I'll be fine. That I get to go to heaven based on the beliefs I was born into, but you can't because of the different beliefs you were born into. That I can prosper at the expense of the planet, but I'll be fine.

Our session today begins by feeling interconnection within the body. Quiet your mind, focus on your breath, and move deeply in the mind-body-breath connection. Feel this connection, then hold it for ten minutes.

Mid-point check-in

Read this sentence out loud but insert your own name: "I exist in no one thing; there is no <u>Chris</u>. I exist in every thing; there is no <u>Chris</u>." Remember our cup that was both broken and not broken, or our drinking glass that had no permanent state? You are no different.

And yet there's a part of you that never dies. Paradoxically, this part doesn't belong to you. You are a single wave in the vast ocean. Can you feel that you're part of the ocean of consciousness? Can you let go of your relentless self-preoccupation and free your mind to connect with something greater than self?

Spend another ten minutes not trying to understand the experience but feeling the part of you that lives in everything. You don't need to understand it intellectually to feel it. In fact, trying to understand it with your everyday mind limits the experience because it exists outside our normal everyday consciousness.

Here's how you can apply this lesson to the rest of your day

Today, without exception, abandon all defensiveness. You're not your opinions or beliefs, so you don't need to defend them. The part of you that you feel the need to defend will die, it is impermanent. It is the part of you that doesn't belong to you that will live on; and it doesn't need you to defend it. Work on letting go of self and moving into a deeper sense of interconnection by abandoning the desire to defend something that is temporary.

Parting quotes

First, a quote from Einstein:

"A human being is a part of the whole called by us 'universe', a part limited in time and space. He experiences himself, his thoughts and feeling as something separated from the rest, a kind of optical delusion of his consciousness. This delusion is a kind of prison for us, restricting us to our personal desires and to affection for a few persons nearest to us. Our task must be to free ourselves from this prison by widening our circle of compassion to embrace all living creatures and the whole of nature in its beauty."

Second, below are several quotes from the Upanishads, a text by unknown authors written at least 2000 years ago. How did these ancient yogis come to understand what modern science through quantum physics and neuroscientists are just beginning to understand? By observing their own bodies and minds.

"…to realize the unity of life. Those who realize that all life is one are at home everywhere and see themselves in all beings"

"Where one realizes the indivisible unity of life, sees nothing else, hears nothing else, knows nothing else, that is the Infinite"

"Wake up from this dream of separateness"

"Only when we pierce through this magic veil do we see the One who appears as many"

"…all forms of life are one"

Day 12

Questioning Enlightenment

The key lesson in today's session is to question 'enlightenment' so that it doesn't become an unobtainable dream, but something that you can grasp in any given moment.

Building from the last session we are careful not to escape one belief, like the paradigm of separation, only to become ensnared in a false perception of what enlightenment means. As your meditation practice deepens, you'll become increasingly aware of beliefs that limit your happiness and often create suffering. To find freedom we cannot substitute one false belief for another. Continuing from the last session where we experientially understood interconnection to escape the paradigm of separation, today we question enlightenment and what it means.

Have you ever asked yourself: What is enlightenment? Does it even mean anything? Without questioning it many of us assume it is heaven on earth, where we find freedom from all suffering and are in a constant state of bliss and joy. This is problematic for at least three reasons. First, our experience of happiness is dependent on knowing suffering. Second, suffering is a necessary part of everyone's life. For example, it's why a baby cries and why someone might decide they're ready to die. Why rob ourselves of suffering and all its powerful lessons? How can we rise above our suffering if we never suffer? As the saying goes: Smooth seas do not make strong sailors. Third, as any drug addict or pharmacist will tell you, our bodies are remarkably adaptive. You would require a continuously higher dosage of happiness to feel it to the same extent as before. It would never be enough.

Therefore, enlightenment can't be complete freedom from suffering. More realistically, we can perceive it as enjoyment without attachment; suffering without aversion, and something to be experienced in moments rather than lifetimes.

In today's session see if you can experience enlightenment defined as just one moment when you're free from attachment and desire, as well as aversion and suffering. You must bring the mind to total stillness, but only for a moment. Once there, feel the happiness that floods your body, but don't get carried away by it, don't attach to it or seek more of it. Just hold your mind in stillness, feel it knowing that it will pass shortly. Work at this for ten minutes.

Mid-point check-in

Someone once asked the Buddha skeptically, "What have you gained through meditation?" The Buddha replied, "Nothing at all." The questioner then, almost mockingly said: "Then, Blessed One, what good is it?" Buddha patiently responded: "Let me tell you what I lost through meditation: anger, depression, insecurity, the burden of old age and sickness, the fear of death. That is the good of meditation, which leads to nirvana."

This story tells us that in enlightenment we still get sick, we still age, we still die. What has been obtained is that these realities are no longer something to be feared; no longer burdens; only accepted realities that we all must face. There's nothing wrong with you if you get sick; you're not atoning for past karma; you're not weak. Everyone gets sick, it's part of life and it's our bodies adapting and responding to viral or bacterial threats. You cannot know health without illness, strength without weakness. There's a time for health and there's a time for illness. Finding freedom not in the delusion of permanent health and strength, but by freeing yourself from attachment and aversion. We can use a famous Japanese haiku to answer what is enlightenment?

Insects on a branch, floating downstream, still singing.

Continue as before for the next ten minutes. Still the mind completely, even if just for a few moments, and experience our definition of enlightenment.

Here's how you can apply this lesson to the rest of your day

Two things to work on today: Don't create any new attachments or aversions and overcome those that already exist. When you're enjoying something, rather than seeking more of it, enjoy it as it is right now, knowing that it's subject to change. For example, if you're enjoying a drink with your friends, know when to stop. Maybe you don't need more, finding contentment with what you've already consumed, or perhaps you find greater joy in a single drink knowing that any more will result in diminishing returns of happiness. When you're not enjoying something, rather than running from it, try to experience it without aversion. For example, you could clean the washroom without disgust, trying to perceive the entire experience neutrally. See for yourself that when you cut your attachments and aversions you reduce suffering and create happiness.

Parting quote

"Before enlightenment, chop wood and carry water. After enlightenment, chop wood and carry water." - Zen saying

Day 13

There's Value in Suffering

The key lesson in today's session is that there's value in suffering, and it's therefore not something we should always try to avoid or run from. When we're at our lowest point, we have the most potential for growth.

Building from previous sessions we'll continue to question false beliefs like separation or that suffering is something to always be avoided. You've come to understand that suffering is largely self-created through our attachments and aversions. In today's practice we learn that while we seek to reduce our suffering, when it inevitably comes, we don't need to approach it with aversion, not only because the experience is impermanent, but also because it's valuable.

Alchemy is rooted in Gnosticism which offers a different interpretation of the teachings of Jesus. These beliefs were heavily suppressed until the discovery of the Dead Sea Scrolls in Nag Hamadi Egypt in 1946. A Latin word that came from Alchemy that we don't have in English is *Nigredo*. *Nigredo* is a dark time, a time of suffering, often symbolized with a monk in a cave. It's an internal, dark, cave-like experience from which we as individuals must emerge. What's different about this word is the recognition that there's value in the darkness, that it's often in times of suffering that we find our greatest insights. Just as we heard that English has around twenty words to describe greed, we see that it lacks a word to describe the value in suffering; a linguistic bias against suffering.

As noted, the experience of *Nigredo* is often depicted as a monk in a dark cave, and above him are seven stars, which represent the value that's gained from spending time in suffering. Take a few moments to test this idea yourself; when you've suffered have you also gained something valuable? You'll likely come to see that life's struggles are like the thorns on a rose; without the thorns, there would be no rose. First come the thorns, and only then can the rose bloom.

Imagine you're on a solo hike through a forest. The smells are intoxicating and refreshing. The wind in the trees holds your attention. Listening to the leaves blowing you look up and are dazzled by the reflections of light through the trees. Not paying attention to where you're walking, you trip and fall into an old abandoned well!

Beyond a few annoying bruises and cuts you're not hurt. You look for a way to climb out only to make several fruitless attempts. You begin to panic, but panic can't help you get out. Realizing this eventually, you sit down and close your eyes. You sit there for hours, occasionally yelling for help to no avail. Your suffering increases. You're hungry and your water bottle is almost empty. Yelling has only worsened your thirst. This goes on for three days. Then things get worse. A terrible storm comes through, soaking and frightening you. At one point the storm is so bad a tree is blow over and falls partly into the well. It's dark and hard to see and you've been cut on the face by the branches. You cry as you have every day while trapped in the well, unsure if you'll survive.

But then the storm passes, the clouds clear. Looking up from the bottom of the well you see seven stars. For a few moments they clear your mind and you realize your suffering has passed. With the light from the stars you see that the fallen tree has given you a way out of the well. You climb the precariously fallen tree and manage to escape.

Having emerged from this terrible experience, what might you have learned? For a little while at least, you'll really appreciate what you drink and eat, feeling very grateful. You'll love your friends and family and even strangers more. You'll have learned that you can suffer more than you realized, going without food or companionship for days. The hours alone may have taught you something about yourself and your thought patterns. In the end, your time in the well will give you powerful life lessons.

This mental image of *Nigredo* demonstrates that there's value in suffering. For the next ten minutes create the story above in your mind and neutrally observe the bodily sensations and thoughts that arise. Experience the sensations of being trapped, cold, alone, hungry and tired. Just you and your thoughts, deep in a well.

Mid-point check-in

In the 1980's in an American desert, scientists created a bio-dome experiment where they built what they thought was the perfect eco-system. For years things went well; the trees grew tall, the vegetables thrived, the humans that lived there for months at a time loved it. But then one day a tree fell, and then another, and another, and so on. At first, the scientists were baffled. Eventually they figured out that because there was no wind, no resistance, there was no need for the roots of the trees to grow deep, so when they grew tall, they simply fell over. Embrace the wind, grow deep and strong roots during your struggles, and importantly feel grateful for the difficulties and how they can positively change you.

For the next ten minutes rather than clearing your mind think of all the times you've suffered. Imagine that each time you suffered, your roots, stability, and strength grew. See for yourself the value in suffering.

Here's how you can apply this lesson to the rest of your day

Today notice all the times you avert from suffering in increasingly subtle ways. Don't allow these opportunities for insight to pass you by. Think of the word *Nigredo* and remind yourself of the value in suffering. Lean into any suffering you find, whether self created or not, like you would an invaluable life lesson. You can even extend the lesson to getting older. Aging isn't something to be ashamed of or embarrassed about, it's a teacher telling us what's important and where to devout your time and energy.

Parting quotes

"Neurosis is always a substitute for legitimate suffering" - Carl Jung

"There is only one thing that I dread: not to be worthy of my sufferings." - Dostoevski

Day 14

Embracing a Lack of Purpose to Find Greater Presence

The key lesson in today's session is to question your belief in purpose to create greater presence.

Building from previous sessions we'll continue to question our worldview to create greater freedom in our lives through presence. In this lesson we question the idea of a life's purpose, and while empirical research has found benefits to a belief in purpose, we'll take a contrasting perspective as we examine how a belief in purpose can blind us to what's right in front of us.

There are an estimated 100 billion stars in our galaxy, and 100 billion galaxies, and this in only one universe, let alone the multiverse that many scientists now believe exists. With this broad topography we can perceive ourselves as nothing more than a collection of ants under a rock hanging out in corner of the Milky Way. In the vastness of the cosmos can we really believe that we [as individuals or as species] have a purpose? Further, no matter who you are or what you achieve in life, at some point everyone is forgotten. Even Jesus and Buddha will be forgotten eventually.

Rather than feeling sad or disconcerted by our lack of purpose, you can use it to create greater presence. If, in considering the size of the cosmos and the history of the planet we cannot reasonably expect our puny existence to have a purpose, then what are we to do? Well, one answer, is that we can find personal meaning within every moment. The legacy of what you do in your life will always, eventually, be nil, therefore, what matters is now. Rather than seeking a long-term extension of self, finding comfort in a false perception of immortality and delusional importance, seek a deep experience in each moment, because that's all you have.

Practice this for the next ten minutes by enjoying the present moment exactly as it is. Find that in freeing yourself from the desire for purpose, you also free yourself from the need to feed your ego in the present and extend it into the future, allowing you to move more deeply into this moment exactly as it is without attachment or aversion, then the next moment, then the next.

Mid-point check-in

Become increasingly aware of your unconscious mental habits, especially as it relates to purpose. See all the ways you try to create purpose for yourself in this life, then free yourself of that desire. Every time you do that, observe if the abandonment of the need for purpose creates greater presence. Even if you are currently doing something incredible, something admired by millions of people such that generations from now people will still know your name, see that a preoccupation with your future self robs you of your ability to fully enjoy the present.

Observe your thoughts without getting caught in their karmic net for the next ten minutes.

Here's how you can apply this lesson to the rest of your day

Try to live at least one day, today, without the need or desire for long term purpose. When it arises, let it go. Spend the day finding purpose not in an extension of ego, but in its abandonment, creating a depth of experience and presence. If you're drinking a warm cup of coffee, let that be your purpose. With your children, let that be your purpose. Whatever you're doing at work right now, let that be your purpose. Today, find purpose in every moment through the depth of your presence.

Parting quote

"Without desire everything is sufficient.

With seeking myriad things are impoverished.

Plain vegetables can soothe hunger.

A patched robe is enough to cover this bent old body.

Alone I hike with a deer.

Cheerfully I sing with village children.

The stream under the cliff cleanses my ears.

The pine on the mountain top fits my heart." - Ryokan

Week Two Complete

You've now completed two weeks of meditation and are close to creating a new, hopefully lifelong habit. In the past week you've come to recognize: that it takes tremendous courage to allow ourselves to be vulnerable; how an understanding of impermanence can help us avoid the creation of our own suffering; how our desires can create suffering; that a deep, experiential understanding of interconnection can help us make the world a better place; that enlightenment can be obtainable if we seek it in moments rather than lifetimes; there's value in suffering so we don't need to try to avoid it; and that rather than constantly seeking a purpose in an ever expanding cosmos we can instead find purpose in what we're doing right now.

By experiencing these paradigm shifts within your own body you don't need to believe what you're being told, you can feel them for yourself. This also means that all responsibility for self change lies with you. It's not your external circumstances or the lessons necessarily, but your own efforts and experiences. This is why many pictures show Buddha on clouds in the sky pointing to the moon, telling us that it's not him, but the path that must be followed.

Hopefully the insights you've gained from your own hard and persistent work have helped you reduce your suffering and increase your happiness, finding more freedom each day. All in only two weeks!

As we move into our third and final week you may feel excited as you near the completion of your "21-day Meditation Challenge". Excitement is a wonderful experience and just as there's no need to push it away, be careful not to attach to such an impermanent sensation. Experiencing it now without aversion or attachment creates freedom when it inevitably dissipates and is replaced by another sensation, which can be equally valued.

In this final week we push your meditation practice to the thirty minute goal. Make sure you give yourself this time to move deeply into the final seven meditation sessions for week three.

As always, we'll continue to build on what you've already done. With some ability to quiet the mind we'll move deeper into listening; we'll discover an unlimited capacity for happiness that's always available if you can quiet your thoughts and the suffering that they can bring. We'll learn to use our meditation practice as time spent feeling whole and perfect exactly as we are; start to understand our dark sides and how through acceptance and assimilation of our shadow we can reduce suffering and increase happiness. In addition, we'll explore the full extent of free will and choice that will allow us to take responsibility for our own suffering and happiness. We'll experience non-duality in the body to understand the falsity of simplistic dualisms, and in our final meditation, we'll become aware of the tendency to create separation and expand our egos after personal development. Enjoy this final week!

Day 15

Listening Takes Practice

The key lesson in today's session is that listening is a tremendously valued skill that requires cultivation.

Building from the last session we will use our increasing ability to quiet the mind and just listen. Finding union not by forcing yourself, your opinions, likes and dislikes on others, but by the abandonment of self through active listening. As the Tao Te Ching tells us: "The wise do not hold opinions. They are aware of the needs of others." And also: "Those who know do not talk. Those who talk do not know."

We all value someone who's a good listener, yet most of us struggle to be this person. We often spend more time talking about ourselves than listening to others. We're thinking about what we'll say next rather than focusing and caring for the person that's speaking to us.

Take a moment to reflect on how you feel when speaking to someone who is an excellent listener. Now, as a contrast, compare that to when you've spoken to someone and you can see they aren't listening. Perhaps they're distracted or just impatiently waiting to speak again themselves. Which person do you want to become? One requires hard work, but the reward is we learn new things and fully experience the moment. The other, no work at all and no reward other than perhaps selfish and temporary gratification.

We miss much when we fail to listen. Not only what the person is saying, but all the non-verbal cues from body language, tone, gestures, eye movement, how what they're saying out loud is not actually how they feel. What they're saying is a projection of themselves and can give us insight into their thought process, if we tune in completely. They might be waiting for a specific and important response from us. Listening well is an opportunity to escape ourselves, our biases and judgments, and to step, as much as possible, into the world of another. We should be in awe of the power of listening, not just when we see it in others but when we experience it with ourselves.

Being a great listener isn't limited to listening to other people. Mother Nature has much to communicate, too. The wind speaks of change, the water reflects our projections, the trees impart acceptance, animals teach us of suffering and freedom, and our own bodies tell us how to move safely and what's good or bad for us. What else can you learn from Mother Nature? Listen intently for yourself. If you're in a place where you can't listen to the outdoors, just listen to your breath or heartbeat.

For the next fifteen minutes improve your ability to listen by stopping the persistent mental noise of the mind. Quiet the mind by focusing on your breath for as long as you can. When the mind inevitably wanders, patiently and persistently come back to your breath.

Mid-point check-in

Use the following as inspiration: The wind whispers its secrets through the leaves of a great walnut tree. I can't tell if it's the wind that speaks or my projections. I must listen more intently until I vanish, and all that remains is Mother Nature's voice, and Mother Nature shining brightly within me.

For the next fifteen minutes imagine traveling to a new mental space where you, as you normally perceive yourself, don't exist, only the sounds around or within you. You can envision this as activating a different part of your brain if that helps. Notice that your egotistical self and its relentless thoughts aren't permitted in this new space. You must abandon it for this trip, otherwise you can't even walk out the front door.

Here's how you can apply this lesson to the rest of your day

Talk very little today, both verbally and mentally. Spend as much of the rest of your day listening as possible. Remember how broad listening is, and that it can include nonverbal cues, nature and your own body. Who knows what secrets you might learn?

Parting quotes

"The word 'listen' contains the same letters as the word 'silent'." - Alfred Brendel

"There's a lot of difference between listening and hearing." - G. K. Chesterton

"It's not at all hard to understand a person; it's only hard to listen without bias." - Criss Jami

"I tried to discover, in the rumour of forests and waves, words that other men could not hear, and I pricked up my ears to listen to the revelation of their harmony." - Gustave Flaubert

Day 16

Quieting the Mind to Discover Happiness

The key lesson in this session is that our minds have been allowed to run wild and it takes time and patience to create space between thoughts. As we improve our capacity to not think, we increase our ability to experience happiness within a given moment. Lengthening the space between thoughts, we find a well of happiness that has no bottom.

Building from previous sessions you'll work at expanding the space you've been able to create between your thoughts, while not attaching to them as they arise. This will allow you to further increase happiness.

Often when we discuss our minds or brains, we're referring to the intellectual side, yet the mind is much richer than this narrow conceptualization. Flow can be described as a mental space with little thought; a sustained state of presence in the body and mind. If you've ever attained a state of flow you know that in quieting the intellectual mind another version of mind can take control and you move more efficiently and effectively.

Today, spend time exploring this other aspect of mind, finding peacefulness and understanding in the rich emptiness of mind. Thanks to neuroscientists we're beginning to understand the brain more, although we still know little about the interconnections within. For this session, imagine that your intellectual mind is out of the driver's seat and has moved to the back seat. And in the meantime, the intuitive mind has moved from the back seat into the driver's seat.

Work at this by trying to think of nothing for the next fifteen minutes. Don't try to forcefully stop thoughts that arise, just don't attach to the thoughts. Allow them to float by like clouds in the sky, as you did in the first week. Get better at doing this: observing the thoughts without getting caught in the karmic net of additional thoughts.

Mid-point check-in

Are you thinking right now? Your goal in this session isn't to stop the thoughts, but to not attach to them as they arise. Allow the thoughts to arise, but don't get caught in them. Patiently and persistently come back to not thinking and for the next fifteen minutes. See how you feel when you find this space in the mind. You're putting effort into not thinking, not to obtain mastery of mind, but to liberate it.

Here's how you can apply this lesson to the rest of your day

Time how long you can go without attaching to a thought. How do you do this? Look at the clock, then you can either close your eyes or keep them open depending on what you normally do when you meditate. Keep a clear mind as long as you can but remember that thoughts are permitted, we're simply trying not to attach to them. Inevitably, once you get caught in a pattern of thoughts and snap out of it, look at the clock to see how long you've gone without attaching or getting caught in your thoughts. Do this for as long as you'd like. At the end of the day record your best time and seek to improve it tomorrow.

As you free yourself from relentless thinking and you temporarily disrupt the endless flow of thoughts, observe how you feel. You might find limitless creativity, joy, peace, compassion, and love; all within your own mind. See for yourself that you can free yourself from suffering by not thinking, and in this quiet and unlimited space you find happiness. Notice that this happiness is always available to you, you just need to quiet the mind so you can experience it.

Parting quotes

"I have lived on the lip of insanity, wanting to know reasons, knocking on a door. It opens. I've been knocking from the inside." - Rumi

"A disciplined mind brings happiness." - Buddha

"You have power over your mind - not outside events. Realize this, and you will find strength." - Marcus Aurelius

"Happiness is a habit—cultivate it." - Elbert Hubbard

"We master the world by mastering our self." - Zeno of Citium

Day 17

Feeling Whole

The key lesson in today's session is that your meditation practice gives you time to feel whole and complete exactly as you are.

Building from previous sessions we'll continue to question what most of us have been taught through an experiential understanding of the body and mind. We examine a common but often unintentionally harmful belief that you're never good enough.

Examine your own upbringing and life to see if this is true. Have you always sought to become something more? Did your parents always push you to be more than you are? They likely had good intentions but still the message was there, that you were never enough as you were. More money, more education, more recognition, more accomplishments, more goals, more relationships and networking, and so on. There's even a concept called spiritual materialism, where we seek to gain more spiritually. The Buddha reportedly said that the ambitious man will always be inferior. Why? Because the ambitious person is never content with what they have, they are always lacking no matter what they've achieved.

Of course goals, financial success, education, healthy relationships, spiritual progress, and so on, are all valuable. But in this session, we give ourselves a break from our endless pursuits. We let go of our constant desire for more, even if just for thirty minutes, and feel whole and perfect exactly as we are.

For the next fifteen minutes imagine that you've already accomplished everything, nothing is missing! There's nothing to be gained, nothing to add, just uproot your desire for more. Sit in perfect and complete contentment and see for yourself if your happiness grows.

Notice that the growth in happiness comes not from the obtainment of your goals, but once again, in their abandonment.

Mid-point check-in

Alan Watts said that the only people who should plan for the future are the ones that know how to live in the present. Otherwise even in the future, you'll still be thinking of the future because you haven't trained yourself to live in the present.

Spend the remaining fifteen minutes training to live in the present with complete contentment. This could be the best investment you could make in your future. As you meditate, whenever the mind wanders gently remind yourself that there's nothing to gain, nothing you need to add. You've returned to the Garden of Eden and it was always available to you, you just needed to leave your ambition at the gate.

Here's how you can apply this lesson to the rest of your day

Spend the rest of your day seeking contentment with the way things are, rather than how you want them to be. Do this especially with yourself. Much of our life is spent feeling inadequate, that we need to be and have more. Today, give yourself and everything around you a break. Put effort into perceiving everything around you as perfect. See how this change in perspective impacts your relationships with other people, animals, nature and perhaps most importantly to yourself.

Parting quote

"Only those who have cultivated the art of living completely in the present have any use for making plans for the future, for when the plans mature they will be able to enjoy the results." - Alan Watts

"It is better to travel well than to arrive." - Buddha

Day 18

Shadow Work

The key lesson in today's practice is that we need to accept all parts of ourselves, even the darkest shadow, and this acceptance leads to compassion for ourselves and others.

Building from previous sessions we'll learn that our judgments are often projections of the parts of ourselves that we haven't yet accepted. As we accept what we perceive as the worst parts of ourselves, we can uproot many of our judgments of ourselves and others.

Have you ever witnessed yourself perceiving a tree? The Indian philosopher Krishnamurti noted that our tendency is to focus on the most beautiful parts of the tree. Perhaps it's a magnolia tree with beautiful flowers in the spring. We focus on the flowers and the green on the leaves. What we tend not to perceive, are the dead branches or rotting leaves. It's the same with ourselves. We focus on the pretty parts and ignore the parts we don't like, or vice versa. But for our personal growth we must perceive the entire tree, or our entire selves.

The great psychoanalyst Carl Jung believed that 'shadow work' was our most important task for consciousness development. He conceived of the shadow as an archetype of the dark side of a person's personality, something we all posses. Rather than attempting to repress our shadow as many religions teach us to do, Jung preached acceptance and assimilation. Without this, the shadow remains in our projections and often in dreams.

Consider the following: The name Lucifer, our most common projection of shadow, means light bearer, and light shines brightest in the dark. Evil is live spelled backwards, and while you can't live without evil you can change how you perceive it. Attempts at punishing or repressing evil simply prolong it. Only through acceptance and love can we gain control over our shadow rather than the shadow controlling us.

For the next fifteen minutes, think of the parts of yourself that you don't like. For example, perhaps you don't like your anger. Try to locate anger in your body. Is it in your gut? Your chest? Anywhere. Now rather than repressing it or distracting yourself from it, hold to the experience of anger in your body. Learn that you can hold it, and you don't need to push it out and share it with others as you've already done in an earlier meditation practice. Remember that the word emotion originates from the Latin "to move out." See for yourself that you don't need to move it out, you can hold it. You might also try other emotions typically perceived as negative like hatred, fear, confusion, etc. Accept them as part of who you are.

Mid-point check-in

Now that you've realized your capacity to hold the shadow manifested as "negative" emotions, spend the next fifteen minutes loving these parts of yourself. Again, find the emotion in the body, hold it, then love it. Find that in first accepting the emotion, then loving it, it dissipates. Feel this happen in your body to further your understanding of the process.

This might lead you to the profound realization that pushing the emotion out only serves to ensure its survival. Holding and loving our emotions, however, not only means that it dissolves within yourself, but you no longer share it with others.

Here's how you can apply this lesson to the rest of your day

Continue your shadow work for the rest of the day in the following two ways. First, use what you learned in today's meditation practice with any "negative" emotion. For example, if someone cuts you off in traffic, locate your anger in the body, most likely in the gut, hold it instead of pushing it out by swearing, yelling, or getting aggressive. You've already proven that you have the capacity to hold it in your body. Once you have a firm hold of it, you might envision hugging it, then witness it disintegrate. It doesn't have to spread in your body and be shared with others. As we'll explore in our next meditation practice, you can choose what you do with the anger: love it and it disintegrates, or spread it.

Second, notice that as you begin to accept your shadow, you more readily see the shadow in others. This is yet another powerful result of a consistent meditation practice. As we further our own self-awareness, particularly through shadow work, we come to understand ourselves better, and the result is we understand others better as well.

This deep, experiential understanding of our accepted shadow then allows us to examine and witness the shadow of others with compassion rather than judgment and condemnation for what we really fear most deeply about ourselves. The perception of evil is but a lack of compassion, for self and other. The belief in an externalized evil is a projection of what you fear and cannot accept within yourself. Once you see and accept the "monster" or Hyde within yourself, it no longer controls you.

Parting quotes

"What if I should discover that the poorest of the beggars and the most impudent of offenders are all within me; and that I stand in need of the alms of my own kindness, that I, myself, am the enemy who must be loved – what then?" - Carl Jung

"For evil arises in the refusal to acknowledge our own sins." - M. Scott Peck

"When there is no enemy within, the enemies outside cannot harm you." - African Proverb

"We can never obtain peace in the outer world until we make peace with ourselves." - Buddha

Day 19

Taking Responsibility for Our Suffering and Happiness: It's a Choice

The key lesson in today's meditation is that we don't often exercise our freedom of choice to its full extent because we tend to be lazy.

Building from previous sessions we'll continue to see how we are often the cause of our suffering and can equally be the cause of our happiness.

The army psychiatrist Scott Peck believed that laziness and narcissism were the root of human evil. The evil of laziness is pernicious and can be obscured. In many situations we're apt to blame other people for how we feel rather than taking ownership. For example, when driving if someone makes us angry, we blame them. They're the idiot who doesn't know how to drive. They are the cause of our anger. Yet why would we choose to give someone this power of us, ever? The power to decide how we feel. Instead, we should first take responsibility for the anger, that we allowed it to grow, we nurtured it. You know now that it starts as a small sensation in the body, and you have the choice to hold and love it, or to spread it.

Once we take responsibility, we have ownership over how we feel. We take back the power of our own feelings and emotions by overcoming our laziness to displace the cause, and thus effort to change it, to someone else. It's much more work to take responsibility for your anger when someone cuts you off and you almost get in an accident, but you maintain power over yourself rather than giving it away.

Today, purposely meditate somewhere that's noisy. It doesn't have to be excessively noisy, but loud enough that you initially find it annoying. Commit to sitting through the noise. Neutrally observe how often the mind wants to blame whoever or whatever is making the noise. You might find yourself saying something like: Why are they always cutting their grass right when I'm meditating? Does the music or a person's voice have to be that loud? This loudmouth is clearly a fool who can't stop talking about themselves as though anyone cares. Observe the stories the mind tends to make up without getting caught in the thoughts.

For the next fifteen minutes, repeatedly take ownership of whatever you're feeling, maybe anger, annoyance, irritability, tension. You are the cause of these feelings, not the noise, because you're choosing to allow them to bother you through a failure to accept things as they are. You can free yourself of these feelings at any time, it's your choice. Explore your full potential of choice.

Mid-point check-in

As we increasingly realize that we have control over our suffering and happiness, we can begin to exercise our choice in more subtle ways. Did your partner forget to take out the trash while you were away? You have total control over your reaction and if that reaction is anger, you've decided to be angry and your partner didn't make you angry. Did you come home to a messy house that was supposed to be clean? Nobody is making you react to the situation poorly but yourself. You can express disappointment in a calm way, that choice is yours. Did someone steal from you? Don't let them also steal your peace of mind or who you want to be.

There's a story that the Buddha once came to a village and taught his noble eightfold path. The wife of a wealthy merchant became a convert. Over a couple weeks so too did many of his workers. They all left their jobs and decided to follow the Buddha. The merchant was angry and believed the cause of his anger was the Buddha, so he sought to kill him.

One day while the Buddha was meditating, the merchant approached him with vengeance and malevolence in his eyes. With a clear mind the Buddha was able to notice this nonverbal cue and said:

"No. I see the gift you hope to give me, and I don't accept it. You're responsible for your own anger. You can either keep it and leave or stay and I'll teach you how to let it go." Witnessing the Buddha's insight and compassion the merchant lost his anger and accepted the offer to stay.

Whenever you allow the negative emotions of someone else to affect you, remember this story. It's your choice whether you want to accept it from them or not. You can say no. Even in an argument with your partner, who might be yelling at you, if you yell back or get caught in anger, that's your choice. Once you recognize this and work at not accepting a harmful gift from someone else, you are guaranteed to reduce your suffering and increase your happiness.

For the last fifteen minutes continue to take ownership for how you're feeling and increase your awareness of the continuous choices you're making.

Here's how you can apply this lesson to the rest of your day

Spend the day recognizing the power of choice. See how often you can take ownership of your feelings and current situation, and that you have a choice of how you want to react. Perhaps you're in a yoga class and the person beside you is loud, not following the teacher's instructions, and falling frequently and dramatically. Recognize that you have a choice to be annoyed, or to accept things as they are.

There are strategies that can help you with these situations, like telling yourself that you don't know this person's situation or what they're currently going through. But avoid speculation, and just focus on what you have control over, your own feelings, thoughts and reactions. Today, explore the full range of the freedom of choice.

Parting quotes

"Know this: Enlightenment and freedom are not arbitrarily handed down. They are the result of intentional effort." - Lao Tzu

"It's not that I'm so smart, it's just that I stay with problems longer." - Einstein

"The recovery of your sick, or the return of your absent friend, or some other favorable event, raises your spirits, and you think good days are preparing for you. Do not believe it. Nothing can bring you peace but yourself." - Ralph Waldo Emerson

"Holding on to anger is like grasping a hot coal with the intent of throwing it at someone else; you are the one who gets burned." - Buddha

"Let nothing perturb you, nothing frighten you. All things pass. God does not change. Patience achieves everything." - Saint Teresa of Avila

Day 20

Experiencing Non-Duality in the Body to Better Understand Reality

The key lesson in today's session is that dualistic thinking is simplistic and often incorrect. While seeing the world in black and white makes it ostensibly easier to understand, reality is too complex and interconnected to conform to a dualistic perspective.

Building from previous sessions we continue to question paradigms by feeling their falsity in the body, then changing our perspectives accordingly.

A yin and yang symbol shows the interconnection between all dualities and uses black and white colours to do so. Yin is often black and yang white, but each also contains a dot of the other in this increasingly ubiquitous symbol. You cannot have one without the other.

Let's feel this in the body. Become aware of your breath. Deepen the inhales and exhales but not excessively so. As your awareness comes to your breath, you're likely to feel calm. Continue to breath into this calmness.

Now become aware of the energy that rests just below your navel. Bring all your awareness to this space where some say there's a sleeping or blind Buddha within us all. Feel the energy there. Don't flex this part of your body or move at all, just bring your awareness to the energy that radiates from this space.

Now simultaneously hold some awareness in that space while being aware of your breath. Feel that energy and calmness exist simultaneously in the body. They are not opposite, but complimentary. Two sides of the same coin. Continue to hold your awareness with your breath and the space below your navel for the next fifteen minutes. Don't overthink it as this can create confusion; just experience it which is a higher level of understanding.

Mid-point check-in

Meditating in stillness, imagine a calm lake surface. Feel that you are this tranquil lake. Now, just as there's much activity below the surface of a serene lake, so too is there much activity under your calm exterior. Become aware of the movement of your heart. Not just its beat but even variation as blood is pumped throughout the heart. Become aware of your gut and the millions of bacteria reproducing, eating, and swimming within you. Become aware of your blood and its constant journey throughout the body, perhaps you can even hear it.

If anyone were to look at you while you were meditating, they would say you're still. And yet, there's tremendous movement within the body. See for yourself that stillness and activity coexist. Continue with this for the remaining fifteen minutes of this meditation.

Here's how you can apply this lesson to the rest of your day

Today, notice all the times you fall into the trap of duality. Perhaps you view the weather as good or bad, rather than allowing for the full variation of weather in a day when it can be both. Perhaps you view your day as good or bad, but really both exist, and you might experience the bad for only a few minutes, yet you allow it to taint your entire day because of your belief in duality. There are thousands of ways duality can creep into your day. Be aware of when it happens and drop this simplistic and false interpretation of our complex reality. See for yourself that there's freedom in escaping the false perception of duality, where things can be as they are without this narrow conceptualization.

Finally, at some point in the day recognize that while you can't escape your own perceptions even though you can change them, you can still feel part of something beyond your individual self. You are an individual wave, but just as the wave is never apart from the ocean, so too are you never apart from something much greater than the self. You are both the wave and the ocean.

Parting quotes

"The world outside your skin is just as much you as the world inside: they move together inseparably…" - Alan Watts

"The path to enlightenment from this world is nothing other than this world itself." - Saichi

Day 21

Avoiding the Dark Side of Personal Development

The key lesson in this final meditation is to avoid the dark side of newly gained knowledge and belief, where you use them to create separation between yourself and others.

Building from the last sessions we seek to avoid freeing ourselves from past false beliefs only to fall back into old thought patterns. The old thought pattern we're seeking to avoid in this final meditation is once again the perception of separation, the creation of "us" who know or believe, versus "them" who are ignorant or lacking faith. As we improve ourselves and change our perspectives, it's easy to believe we are now better than others, and they are somehow less than us because of their perceived ignorance. In this final session we avoid this old thought pattern of separation that creates suffering as we walk the path toward greater happiness and freedom for all.

Having meditated for three weeks and having created a new healthy habit, it's easy to begin to condemn others who aren't consistent with your new knowledge and belief. We must guard against this tendency to put ourselves above others.

For example, you now understand that all things in the world are more connected than they are separate. That dualities are a simplistic interpretation of a complex world where you can both be, and not be, something. You've learned how your desires can create suffering, how to free yourself from suffering through choice, and that when you inevitably suffer there's value. You've come to understand impermanence and that your body is a powerful tool for wisdom and provides an experiential means for you to understand the world. That your or anyone's judgments say more about the person judging than the judged. That our dark side or shadow is to be assimilated rather than repressed, and that this process can give us compassion for ourselves and others.

These are tremendous lessons that will, without fail, reduce your suffering and increase your happiness. Yet as your meditation practice develops, you'll find that your path to greater freedom is riddled with new and old beliefs that aren't helpful. Don't allow an ego inflation from your new knowledge and wisdom. Don't condemn others for perceived ignorance because you've overcome some of your own ignorance.

For the next fifteen minutes feel the connection between your mind, body and breath. Focus on your breath, just as you did in your first meditation twenty days ago. Feel connection within your being. See for yourself that this is the way of the world, interconnection not separation.

Mid-point check-in

On a celebrated religious day, a wise rabbi walked past a young man on the street who was smoking. One this particular day, smoking was forbidden. The rabbi immediately stopped, walked up to the man and said: "Don't you know what today is? That it's a holy day?"

The bold young man replied: "Yes I know what today is." Without pause, he continued to smoke, even blowing smoke toward the rabbi.

Undeterred and without offense, the rabbi sought to be clearer: "And don't you know smoking is forbidden today?"

The unapologetic young man replied: "Yes, I know," as he continued to smoke.

The rabbi smiled, looked up and raised his palms to the heavens and said: "Father, this young man is beautiful, and though he breaks the law on this holy day, he cannot be forced to lie. Remember this on his judgement day, that he could not be forced to lie; that he was a truthful man."

Use your hard work over the last three weeks to see the good in others, just as the rabbi did. For example, instead of seeing ignorance, have compassion and see an opportunity to help them reduce their suffering and increase happiness. Instead of feeling anger or hatred for someone, see them as a powerful teacher reminding you that you control your happiness.

For your final fifteen minutes see the good in yourself. Practice a lack of condemnation or judgment against yourself, so that you might show compassion to others. Feel good for what you've accomplished in your "21 Day Meditation Challenge". Hold to that feeling and spend the next fifteen minutes enjoying it.

Here's how you can apply this lesson to the rest of your day

Bodhisattvas are Buddhists who are said to have passed up nirvana, the end of their suffering, so that they can help others. They believe that humanity cannot be free until everyone is free. Today, feel and observe your compassion for others grow. Be proud of what you've obtained over the last three weeks. Share it with others. But don't fall back into separation. Instead, use what you've worked to obtain to further your connections. Today, catch yourself every time you start to create separation. Come back to the connection between mind, body and breath, feel it, then emanate this connection to everything around you, even if just for a day.

Parting quotes

"Be kind, for everyone you meet is fighting a harder battle." - Plato

"Never discourage anyone...who continually makes progress, no matter how slow." - Plato

"You cannot travel on the path until you become the path itself." - Buddha

"We ourselves feel that what we are doing is just a drop in the ocean. But the ocean would be less because of that missing drop." - Mother Teresa

Conclusion

If you've made it to the end of this book you will have completed all twenty-one days and have created a new, healthy habit. Congratulations! It's hard to imagine a better investment of your time and energy. Your return on investment (ROI) is reduced suffering and increased happiness, not just for you but for those with whom you interact as well. Having come through this experience it will be difficult, and perhaps upsetting, to miss even a day of meditation.

Of course, the hard work isn't done. It will take years and perhaps decades to fully absorb and appreciate many of the lessons shared in this book. Yet such work isn't daunting or something to avert from. Finding joy in the journey, the destination matters less.

Having completed your "21-day Meditation Challenge" you may now wish to return to specific meditations and lessons. Follow any order you want. You might work at some lessons for years, others for only a few days. For maximum benefits put your effort where it is most needed. Work on the weakest parts to strengthen the entirety of your practice.

We conclude by recapping what we've learned over the last twenty-one days.

In our first meditation we focused on our breath in order to stop the relentless turnings of the mind. Here we found respite from the tornado of thoughts that plague us. This was the foundation and first experience that showed how we can often immediately end our suffering by not clinging to thoughts, and experience happiness in the elusive but rewarding emptiness of mind.

We then found motivation to meditate by learning some of the benefits as determined by modern science. We learned that something that is very simple in theory, yet extremely difficult in practice, quieting the mind, can enrich our lives and even change the structure of our brains.

On day three we found that even when we think we're at ease we still maintain some stress in the body. We began to realize that the body is one of our most powerful tools and teachers. This realization allowed us to begin to create ease in the body and mind.

On day four we learned that goals are desires which can, but don't always, create suffering. We found that in letting go of a goal, even if that goal is happiness, we experienced contentment in the present, immediately giving us what we were striving for to begin with, increased happiness. We experienced a beautiful paradox, that in letting go, the goal was achieved. Here we learned what is arguably the most powerful lesson of the Bhagavad Gita, that we must find joy in the work itself, rather than the fruits of the work.

On day five we worked on a Zen concept called Shoshen, beginner's mind. We realized the power of a beginner's mind, always open to the endless possibilities in any given moment. Experts often close themselves off to the wisdom that surrounds them, thinking they already know everything. This limits ourselves and the moment, and we learned to fight against this tendency so that we could stay open to fully enjoy life.

On day six we found that when we experienced freedom from our thoughts, even if only for a few seconds, we had a potentially unlimited capacity for awe and joy. We correspondingly learned that the biggest limit on our happiness and wonder was ourselves.

On day seven, the final day of our first week where we built the foundation of our meditation practice, we began to experience bodily sensations neutrally, without judgment. As we freed ourselves from the judgment of our bodily sensations as good or bad, we took the first experiential steps to realizing that the behavior of others can also be perceived neutrally, without judgment. Freedom from our judgments of others and self is guaranteed to reduce your suffering and increase happiness.

On day eight, the first day of our second week, we began to question the way we viewed the world through bodily experiences. We learned that making ourselves vulnerable takes tremendous courage and wasn't something to be shamed for or ashamed of. While not explicit, we used a story of the Hindu God Shiva laying himself down on a battlefield to stop an out of control Kali. Only by laying himself down before her was Shiva able to pacify Kali. On your deathbed you won't regret the risks you took with your heart; you'll regret the risks you didn't take.

On day nine we bravely confronted our own impermanence, and while it wasn't explicit in the lesson you made progress toward the realization that we need not be afraid of dying, only of not having lived. Recognition of the universal law of impermanence allowed us to see how we create our own suffering by attaching and averting to things that are guaranteed to change. Recognition of your own inevitable death can imbue each moment with greater value.

On day ten we saw how our desires created suffering. Most of us have been taught that happiness is found in the fulfillment of our desires. Yet how can this be true when the desires never end? Happiness is more likely to be found in letting go of our endless desires. The hole within humanity can't be filled with more stuff, whether accomplishments, relationships, money, and so on. The hole can only be filled from within, and a first step is letting go of our desires.

On day eleven we questioned separation and individuality. We learned from the ancient yogis as communicated in the Upanishads, the Yoga-Sutra, and the Bhagavad-Gita that we're all deeply interconnected. We learned the same from modern quantum physics and the study of the connections within our brains and nature. At the root of the greatest existential crises facing humanity is this belief in separation. We felt the falsity of it within our own bodies.

On day twelve we questioned enlightenment, careful not to step into the trap of material spiritualism. Taking enlightenment off an unobtainable podium, we found that we've already experienced it in moments rather than years or lifetimes. Here we had the profound experience that we're both on the path to enlightenment, but also already there.

On day thirteen we learned from the alchemists, those who had to create a symbolic language to escape persecution. We learned of the value of suffering as communicated in the word *Nigredo*. In one meditation session we learned not only can we handle suffering, but that it's a powerful teacher from which we shouldn't run.

On day fourteen, the last day of our second week, we questioned the ubiquitous belief in 'purpose'. While there is a place and benefit to a belief in purpose, we also learned that we aren't dependent on it. We can let it go and find everything we need in this moment, then the next, then the next. Total freedom and completeness, in an instant.

On day fifteen, the first day of our final week where we built on our previous efforts and pushed ourselves even further through hard work and thirty minute sessions, we came to appreciate the value of listening. Listening not just while someone is talking, but to nonverbal cues, our bodies and nature. The lessons to be learned from the space around us while the mind is still are endless. We have an unlimited capacity to listen and thus learn, but only hard work will allow us to explore its depths.

On day sixteen we went further into our unlimited capacities, this time for happiness. We once again found that stillness in the mind produced happiness, but this time we didn't try to stop the thoughts. Instead, we more simply put effort into not getting caught up with them. A small yet powerful nuance that allowed us to go deeper into our endless well of happiness.

On day seventeen we sought to temporarily end our relentless struggle to become more, seeing that our meditation practice can be a time to feel whole. A break from the unrelenting pursuit of self growth. We found that in letting go of our ambition, the goal had already been achieved.

On day eighteen we confronted our shadow, and rather than repress it, we offered acceptance and love. As we assimilated with our shadow as the alchemists and later Carl Jung explained, we gained its knowledge and power, and one result was compassion for the shadows of others.

On day nineteen we explored the full range of choice and found that we can reduce suffering and increase happiness for ourselves and others by taking responsibility for our thoughts and actions. We learned to take back control over our emotions and reactions, recognizing that this power means we have a lot of hard work before us.

On day twenty we moved past the selective and simplistic perception of dichotomies by experiencing non-duality in the body. We simultaneously felt calmness and energy, stillness and activity, the experience of being both the ocean and a single wave. We embraced the rich complexity of reality, rather than a narrow and fearful conceptualization of black and white.

As you improve your ability to see past duality you might re-examine several lessons from this book including that: we are all connected but also separate; desires lead to suffering but can also bring happiness; not thinking is valuable and brings happiness but so can thinking; you can have a purpose and simultaneously not have a purpose; and, that you're perfect as you are but will always have room for improvement.

…and here we are at day twenty-one. On our final day of the challenge we were careful to avoid a common pitfall of self-development where we use our own growth to judge the perceived lack of growth of others. We sought to once again resist the natural urge to create separation, and instead found interconnection with all around us through the abandonment of judgments.

One last story to keep you motivated. The great Tibetan monk Milarepa was nearing the end of his life. He wanted to share his most important secret to success with his best student. The student was very excited to know this lesson. One early morning, Milarepa woke this student and told him to follow him up to the top of a mountain. It was a long and treacherous journey, but the student hardly noticed because he was so excited, and Milarepa contently hiked along, admiring all that was around him. When they finally reached the top of the mountain the student could barely contain himself. Recognizing this, and not wanting the student to suffer any longer, Milarepa said he'd now show his student the secret to his success. He then turned around, pulled down his pants and showed the large calluses on his bum. His secret was just to sit and put in the hard work.

Looking at this summary did you experience and feel all this? Not yet? Don't worry, you have the rest of your life to enjoy working at it.

Manufactured by Amazon.ca
Bolton, ON